A Little Look at Big Reptiles!

Pauline Cartwright

Contents

What Are Reptiles?

Reptiles are animals.
They have scales.
Most reptiles lay eggs.

Reptiles have cold bodies.
They lie in the sun to stay warm.

Some reptiles are little.
Some reptiles are very big.

crocodile

snake

turtle

The Biggest Tortoise

Tortoises are reptiles.
Tortoises cannot walk fast.

This is the biggest tortoise in the world.
This tortoise has a hard shell.
It has a small head and no teeth.

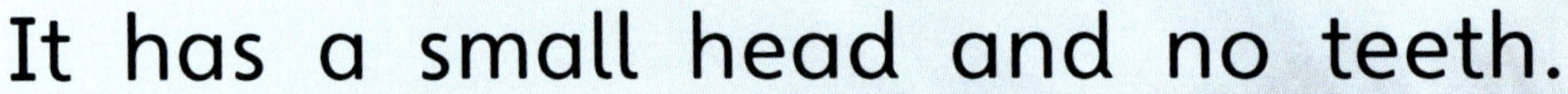

small head

Galapagos tortoise

Name: Galapagos tortoise

Likes: To eat grass and leaves, and sit in the sun

Hates: To walk fast. It is hard with a heavy shell!

hard shell

The Biggest Turtle

Turtles are reptiles.

This is the biggest turtle in the world.
It has big front flippers and can swim fast!

This turtle lives in the sea.
It comes onto land to lay eggs.

Leatherback turtle

Name: **Leatherback turtle**

Likes: To eat jellyfish and squid

Hates: Dry land. It is hard to move on land.

The Biggest Lizard

Lizards are reptiles.

This is the biggest lizard in the world.
It has a long flat head.
Its tail is very long.

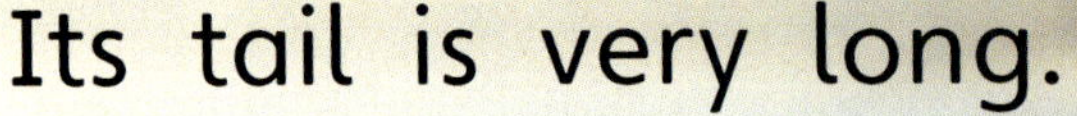

long, flat head

Komodo dragon

Name: **Komodo dragon**

Likes: Climbing trees

Hates: Other Komodo dragons! If it sees one, it will try to eat it!

long tail

The Longest Snake

Snakes are reptiles.

This is the longest snake in the world.
It eats rats, birds and even pigs.

Name: **Regal python**

Likes: To eat rats, birds and other animals

Hates: To chew its food. It swallows animals in one go!

Regal python

The Biggest Reptile

Crocodiles are reptiles.

This crocodile is the biggest reptile in the world.
It can live on land and in water.
It has 65 sharp teeth!

Saltwater crocodile

Name: **Saltwater crocodile**

Likes: To eat monkeys, kangaroos, birds and other animals

Hates: Other crocodiles. It will fight other crocodiles that try to eat its food!

Big to Biggest

Let's see how big these reptiles look when we put them next to each other!

Leatherback turtle

Galapagos tortoise

biggest!

Picture Index